WORK OUTSMART
LEADERSHIP FEARLESS

WOLF

Krikor Karaoghlanian

Dedicated to all the ambitious professionals out there who have the courage to embrace their inner wolf and pursue their career goals with fearless determination. May this book serve as a guide to help you tap into your full potential and lead with strength, empathy, and purpose.

"A wolf doesn't concern himself with the opinions of sheep."

ANONYMOUS

Are you ready to unleash your inner wolf and achieve your career goals like never before?

It takes more than just hard work and talent to succeed.

You need to have the instincts, teamwork, and strategic thinking of a

wolf.

But don't worry, you don't have to howl at the moon or run on all fours to tap into your inner wolf.

Instead, you'll learn how to embody the qualities of a wolf to outsmart the competition and lead fearlessly.

◆ ◆ ◆

In "Work Outsmart Leadership Fearless: WOLF," I'll show you

how to develop a pack mentality in your workplace, leverage your unique strengths, and overcome fear and hesitation to become a more assertive and effective leader. Drawing on my own experiences as well as insights from successful leaders, you'll discover how wolves are known for their intelligence, adaptability, and fierce loyalty to their pack.

Wolves know how to lead, but also how to follow. By embracing your inner wolf, you'll gain the skills and confidence to thrive in any professional setting. Throughout the book, you'll discover the principles and strategies that will help you unlock your full potential and achieve your career goals. Whether you're just starting out in your career or looking to take it to the next level, this book is for you.

So, get ready to discover the wolf within
and start leading fearlessly. It's time
to howl your way to success!

Developing a pack mentality in the workplace is crucial for success because it promotes teamwork, collaboration, and a shared sense of purpose. When employees work together like a pack, they become more than just a group of individuals working towards their own goals.

They become a unified force, working towards a common objective and supporting each other along the way.

A pack mentality creates a positive workplace culture where individuals feel valued, supported, and motivated to perform at their best. When employees feel connected to each other and to their work, they are more likely to be engaged and invested in the success of the team and the organization as a whole.

In addition to promoting teamwork and collaboration, a pack

mentality also helps to foster innovation and creativity. When employees feel comfortable sharing ideas and taking risks, they are more likely to come up with new and innovative solutions to problems.

Developing a pack mentality in the workplace is essential for creating a positive, productive, and successful work environment.

◆ ◆ ◆

A pack mentality in the workplace can foster a sense of teamwork and collaboration, as well as improve communication and decision-making. When everyone on the team is working towards a common goal, and is willing to support and rely on one another, productivity and success are more likely to follow. In contrast, a workplace where individuals operate independently, without considering the impact of their actions on others, can lead to inefficiencies, misunderstandings, and conflict.

We'll Explore The Key Principles Of Developing A Pack Mentality In The Workplace And Provide You With Practical Tools And Strategies To Implement Them Within Your Team. These Strategies Include Building Trust, Promoting Open Communication, Fostering A Sense Of Shared Purpose, And Developing Leadership Skills That Prioritize The Team's Success Over Individual Accomplishments.

◆ ◆ ◆

As you begin to incorporate these principles and strategies into your team's dynamic, you'll likely see an improvement in not only the team's performance but also in the satisfaction and engagement of individual team members.

By working together as a pack, you'll unlock the full potential of your team and achieve success beyond what you could achieve alone.

◆ ◆ ◆

Welcome to our exploration of developing a pack mentality in the workplace! As we delve into the key principles of teamwork and collaboration, we'll equip you with practical tools and strategies to apply these principles within your team.

Building trust is essential to developing a pack mentality in the workplace. Just like wolves communicate and rely on each other for survival, team members must trust each other to work towards a common goal. We'll provide you with strategies for building trust within your team and fostering an environment of mutual respect and support.

Open communication is another crucial component of a pack mentality. Wolves communicate in a variety of ways, and we too must be able to effectively communicate with our colleagues to achieve success. We'll share practical tips and tools for promoting open communication within your team, including active listening, regular check-ins, and honest feedback.

Fostering a sense of shared purpose is also key to developing a pack mentality. Wolves work together towards a common goal - survival - and we too must have a clear sense of purpose and direction within our team. We'll provide you with strategies for defining and communicating a shared purpose within your team, as well as tips for keeping team members motivated and engaged.

Finally, developing leadership skills that prioritize the team's success over individual accomplishments is essential for building a pack mentality in the workplace. Just like the alpha wolf leads and makes decisions for the good of the pack, effective leaders prioritize the success of the team over individual accolades. We'll provide you with strategies for developing leadership skills that foster teamwork and collaboration within your team.

With these practical tools and strategies, you'll be well on your way to developing a pack mentality in the workplace and achieving success as a team.

Let's get started!

Have you ever watched a pack of wolves hunting together?

It's a fascinating display of teamwork and collaboration, as each member of the pack works together towards a common goal - **survival.**

Wolves communicate with each other through body language, vocalizations, and scents, relying on each other's strengths to take down prey and protect their territory.

In many ways, the principles of developing a pack mentality in the natural world can also be applied to the workplace. By fostering a sense of teamwork and collaboration within our teams, we can achieve great things and overcome even the toughest challenges.

◆ ◆ ◆

Building trust is one of the most important aspects of developing a pack mentality in the workplace.

When team members trust each other, they're more likely to communicate effectively and work together towards a common goal. We'll provide you with practical strategies for building trust within your team, including open and honest communication, active listening, and mutual respect.

To build trust within your team, it's important to prioritize open and honest communication. Encourage team members to share their thoughts and ideas openly, and provide regular opportunities for feedback and discussion.

Active listening is also a key component of building trust, so be sure to listen to your team members attentively and demonstrate that you value their input.

Another important aspect of building trust is mutual respect. Treat your team members with respect and empathy, and encourage them to do the same for each other. Acknowledge and appreciate their contributions, and be sure to recognize their accomplishments and successes.

In addition to these strategies, it's important to lead by example when it comes to building trust. Be transparent and honest in your own communication, and demonstrate your commitment to the team's success through your actions. By consistently modeling the behaviors you want to see in your team, you'll build trust and create a more cohesive and collaborative work environment.

◆ ◆ ◆

The first principle, unity of purpose, is all about ensuring that everyone on the team is aligned and working towards the same goal. One strategy for achieving this is to clearly define the team's purpose and communicate it to everyone involved. This could be done through a mission statement, a team charter, or even a simple conversation. It's also important to regularly revisit the purpose and make sure everyone is still on board and working towards it.

Another strategy is to foster a sense of ownership and accountability among team members. When everyone feels like they have a stake in the team's success, they're more likely to work together towards a common goal. One way to do this is to set clear expectations and goals for each team member, and then provide regular feedback and recognition for their contributions.

To illustrate the power of unity of purpose, let's look at the story of a successful team that embraced this principle. The team was working on a complex software development project, and there were many different opinions and ideas about how to approach it. However, the team leader was able to bring everyone together by clearly defining the project's purpose and making sure everyone understood it. This helped the team stay focused and motivated, and they were able to deliver the project on time and with high quality.

The second principle, complementary strengths, is all about leveraging the unique skills and abilities of each team member. One strategy for achieving this is to conduct a skills assessment for each team member and then assign tasks based on their strengths. This helps ensure that everyone is working on tasks that they enjoy and are good at, which can lead to higher job satisfaction and better performance.

Another strategy is to encourage cross-training and knowledge sharing among team members. This helps ensure that everyone has a basic understanding of each other's roles and responsibilities, which can lead to better collaboration and communication.

To illustrate the power of complementary strengths, let's look at the story of a successful team that embraced this principle. The team was working on a marketing campaign for a new product, and each team member had a unique set of skills and experiences. The team leader was able to leverage these strengths by assigning tasks based on each person's expertise, and by encouraging cross-training and knowledge sharing. This helped the team create a well-rounded and effective campaign that generated impressive results.

The third principle, relentless improvement, is all about constantly striving to improve and grow as a team. One strategy for achieving this is to regularly set goals and track progress towards them. This helps ensure that the team is always moving forward and making progress.

Another strategy is to encourage experimentation and risk-taking. When team members feel free to try new things and take risks, they're more likely to come up with innovative solutions and ideas.

To illustrate the power of relentless improvement, let's look at the story of a successful team that embraced this principle. The team was working on a new product development project, and they were struggling to come up with a breakthrough idea. However, the team leader encouraged everyone to think outside the box and try new things, even if they seemed risky or unconventional. This led to a breakthrough idea that ended up being a huge success.

Mutual Support Is A Crucial Component Of Any Successful Team.

When team members feel supported by one another, they are more likely to take risks, be open to feedback, and collaborate effectively. As a leader, you can foster mutual support by creating a culture of psychological safety where team members feel comfortable expressing their opinions and concerns without fear of judgement or retribution.

To further promote mutual support in the workplace, you can encourage team members to offer assistance to each other and collaborate on projects. This could involve pairing up team members with complementary skills or expertise, creating cross-functional teams, or setting up mentorship programs. By doing so, you can help team members learn from each other, build stronger relationships, and develop a sense of shared responsibility for the team's success.

One effective strategy for building mutual support is to hold regular team-building activities and social events. This could include team lunches, happy hours, or even weekend retreats. These activities can help team members get to know each other on a personal level and build stronger bonds that extend beyond the workplace.

Another way to promote mutual support is to recognize and celebrate team members' achievements. This could involve public recognition in team meetings, shout-outs in company newsletters or social media, or even monetary or non-monetary rewards. By recognizing and rewarding team members' contributions, you can reinforce a culture of mutual support and encourage others to do the same.

Ultimately, by fostering mutual support within your team, you can create a more collaborative and productive work environment where everyone feels valued and supported. This can lead to improved morale, higher job satisfaction, and better overall performance.

◆ ◆ ◆

Mutual support is not just about providing assistance in times of need, but also about fostering a culture of collaboration and trust. When team members feel supported and valued by their colleagues, they are more likely to feel motivated and engaged in their work. This can lead to increased productivity, better quality work, and a more positive work environment overall.

One strategy for building mutual support within a team is to encourage open communication and active listening. Team members should feel comfortable sharing their ideas, concerns, and feedback, and should be encouraged to listen actively to their colleagues. This can help to build stronger relationships and create a sense of community within the team.

Another strategy is to create opportunities for team members to collaborate and work together on projects. When team members work together towards a common goal, they are more likely to feel a sense of camaraderie and mutual support. This can be especially beneficial for team members who may be struggling or facing challenges in their work.

Overall, mutual support is a key principle of the pack mentality that can help to build stronger, more cohesive teams. By fostering a culture of collaboration, trust, and support, teams can achieve great things and create a more positive and fulfilling work environment.

Unleash Your Inner Wolf

it's essential to embrace and identify your strengths and weaknesses. Doing so will allow you to work on areas where you need improvement and hone the skills that set you apart.

Here are some ways to identify your strengths and weaknesses:

Self-reflection: Take the time to reflect on your past experiences and your reactions to them. Consider the moments when you felt the most confident and the situations where you struggled the most. Use this self-reflection to identify patterns in your behavior and identify areas where you excel or need to improve.

Feedback: Seek feedback from others, whether it's from friends, family, or coworkers. Listen to their perspectives on your strengths and weaknesses and use this information to gain a better understanding of yourself.

Developing your instincts and intuition is another critical step in unleashing your inner wolf. Your instincts and intuition are natural abilities that can help guide you through tough situations.

Here are some ways to develop your instincts and intuition:

Trust yourself: Trusting yourself means trusting your gut feeling and intuition. Often, we ignore our instincts because we doubt ourselves or lack confidence. When you trust yourself, you'll be more likely to make the right decisions.

Practice mindfulness: Mindfulness is the practice of being present and aware of your surroundings. It allows you to tune into your intuition and develop a deeper sense of awareness.

◆ ◆ ◆

Oercoming Fear And Hesitation Is Crucial To Unleashing Your Inner Wolf. Fear And Hesitation Can Hold You Back And Prevent You From Reaching Your Full Potential.

Here Are Some Ways To Overcome Fear And Hesitation:

Face your fears: Face your fears head-on by confronting them. Taking small steps towards overcoming your fears can help build your confidence and courage.

Take action: Taking action towards your goals, no matter how small, can help you build momentum and overcome hesitation.

Remember, embracing your inner wolf is a journey, not a destination. It takes time, patience, and commitment to unleash your full potential.

Keep pushing yourself to grow, develop, and learn, and you'll be well on your way to unleashing your inner wolf.

remember that every step you take is a step towards becoming your best self. Embracing your strengths and weaknesses, developing your instincts and intuition, and overcoming fear and hesitation are all essential steps that will lead you towards achieving your goals and fulfilling your potential. Keep pushing yourself, even when the road gets tough, and trust in your ability to overcome any obstacle that comes your way. With hard work, dedication, and a fierce determination to succeed, you can unleash the power of your inner wolf and become the best version of yourself.

Lead Like a Wolf

it's essential to learn how to lead like one. Wolves are known for their strong leadership skills, and by embracing their characteristics, you too can become a successful leader.

Here are some key characteristics of successful wolf leaders:

Confidence: Wolf leaders exude confidence, which inspires those around them to follow their lead. They believe in themselves and their abilities, which helps them make tough decisions and take risks.

Clear communication: Wolves communicate with each other using body language, vocalizations, and other nonverbal cues. As a leader, it's essential to communicate clearly and effectively to ensure everyone is on the same page.

Team-oriented: Wolves work together in packs, each with its own role and responsibilities. As a leader, it's essential to create a sense of teamwork and collaboration to achieve common goals.

◆ ◆ ◆

To build trust and respect as a leader, you must establish

credibility with your team.

Here are some strategies for doing so:

Lead by example: Model the behavior you expect from your team. Be reliable, accountable, and transparent.

Listen actively: Listen to your team members' concerns, ideas, and feedback. By actively listening, you show that you value their input and are open to collaboration.

Encourage growth: Provide opportunities for your team members to grow and develop in their roles. This shows that you care about their success and are invested in their future.

Creating a positive and productive workplace culture is essential to unleash your inner wolf as a leader.

Here are some strategies for creating such a culture:

Foster open communication: Create an environment where team members feel comfortable sharing their ideas and opinions. Encourage brainstorming and collaboration to generate new ideas.

Recognize and reward successes: Celebrate your team's accomplishments and recognize individuals for their contributions. This helps create a sense of accomplishment and motivates your team to keep striving for success.

Embrace diversity and inclusivity: Foster an environment where everyone feels valued and respected, regardless of their background or identity. By embracing diversity, you create a more robust and inclusive workplace culture.

◆ ◆ ◆

Competition

To become a successful wolf leader, you need to be able to outsmart the competition. This means developing a strategic mindset, leveraging your unique talents and skills, and being able to innovate and adapt to change.

Strategic Thinking And Planning Are Essential For Any Leader. It Involves Analyzing Your Strengths And Weaknesses, Identifying Opportunities And Threats, And Developing A Plan Of Action To Achieve Your Goals.

Here are some ways to develop strategic thinking and planning skills:

Conduct a SWOT analysis: Identify your organization's strengths, weaknesses, opportunities, and threats. Use this information to develop a plan that leverages your strengths, addresses your weaknesses, and takes advantage of opportunities while mitigating threats.

Set SMART goals: Develop specific, measurable, achievable, relevant, and time-bound (SMART) goals to help you stay focused and motivated.

Develop contingency plans: Anticipate potential obstacles and develop contingency plans to help you overcome them.

Leveraging Your Unique Talents And Skills Is Another Way To Outsmart The Competition. Identify What Makes You And Your Organization Unique And Use It To Your Advantage.

Here are some ways to leverage your unique talents and skills:

Build a diverse team: Create a team with diverse backgrounds, experiences, and perspectives. This will help you approach problems from different angles and come up with innovative solutions.

Focus on your strengths: Identify your strengths and develop them further. This will help you stand out and differentiate yourself from the competition.

Develop a strong brand: Develop a strong brand that reflects your organization's values and unique qualities. This will help you attract and retain customers and employees.

Innovating And Adapting To Change Is Crucial For Outsmarting The Competition. The Business Landscape Is Constantly Evolving, And Leaders Who Can Adapt And Innovate Will Be The Most Successful.

Here are some ways to innovate and adapt to change:

Encourage experimentation: Encourage your team to experiment with new ideas and approaches. This will help you stay ahead of the competition and identify new opportunities.

Embrace new technology: Embrace new technologies and tools that can help you work more efficiently and effectively.

Stay informed: Stay informed about industry trends, emerging technologies, and other factors that could impact your business. This will help you anticipate and respond to changes in the marketplace.

> **By developing strategic thinking and planning skills, leveraging your unique talents and skills, and innovating and adapting to change, you can outsmart the competition and become a successful wolf leader.**

Strategic thinking and planning: Successful leaders know how to analyze their competition and plan accordingly. This involves identifying your strengths and weaknesses, as well as those of your competitors, to develop a strategy that gives you an advantage.

Leveraging your unique talents and skills: Every leader has unique strengths and skills that can be leveraged to outsmart the competition. Identify what sets you apart and find ways to use these qualities to your advantage.

Innovating and adapting to change: Successful leaders know how to adapt to changing market conditions and industry trends. They also know how to innovate to stay ahead of the competition. By continually innovating and adapting, you can maintain a competitive edge.

Understanding your customers: In order to outsmart the competition, you need to understand your customers. This involves understanding their needs, preferences, and behaviors. By understanding your customers, you can develop products and services that meet their needs better than your competitors.

Building a strong team: Your team is a critical component of your success. By building a strong team with diverse skills and perspectives, you can leverage their strengths to outsmart the competition.

Fearless

Being fearless is a crucial aspect of success, as it allows us to take risks and pursue our goals without hesitation. It doesn't mean we don't feel fear, but rather that we don't let it control us.

Fearless leaders are those who are willing to take calculated risks and make tough decisions, even in the face of uncertainty.

They are confident in their abilities and trust themselves to overcome obstacles and challenges.

By embracing fearlessness, we can unlock our full potential and achieve great things.

Remember, courage is not the absence of fear, but rather the willingness to act in spite of it.

Embrace your fears: It's normal to feel fear, but it's how you respond to it that matters. Embrace your fears and use them as motivation to push yourself beyond your limits.

Take calculated risks: Being fearless doesn't mean being reckless. Take calculated risks by considering the potential outcomes and preparing accordingly.

Focus on what you can control: Fear often arises from things that are beyond our control. Instead of worrying about these things, focus on what you can control and take action in those areas.

Practice self-care: Taking care of yourself physically, mentally, and emotionally can help you build resilience and overcome fear.

Surround yourself with positivity: Surrounding yourself with positive people, experiences, and environments can help you maintain a fearless mindset.

Learn from failure: Failure is a natural part of growth and learning. Instead of fearing it, embrace it and use it as an opportunity to learn and improve.

Visualize success: Visualizing success can help you overcome fear and increase your confidence. Picture yourself achieving your goals and focus on the positive outcomes.

being fearless doesn't mean never feeling fear. It means acknowledging your fears and taking action despite them. By embracing your fears, taking calculated risks, focusing on what you can control, practicing self-

care, surrounding yourself with positivity, learning from failure, and visualizing success, you can develop a fearless mindset and achieve your goals.

Career

Your Career Is One Of The Most Significant Aspects Of Your Life. It's Where You Spend Most Of Your Time And Energy, And It Can Have A Profound Impact On Your Personal And Professional Growth. To Succeed In Your Career, You Must Unleash Your Inner Wolf And Tap Into Your Unique Strengths And Abilities.

Here are some ways to discover the wolf within and achieve your career goals:

Embrace Your Unique Talents and Skills: We all have unique talents and skills that set us apart from others. Embracing these talents and skills can help you excel in your career. Take the time to identify your strengths and use them to your advantage

Develop a Growth Mindset: Having a growth mindset means believing that your abilities can be developed through hard work and dedication. By embracing a growth mindset, you'll be more willing to take on new challenges and learn from your mistakes.

Take Calculated Risks: Taking calculated risks can help you achieve your career goals faster. Identify the risks that are worth taking and take the necessary steps to mitigate them.

Don't Be Afraid to Fail: Failure is a natural part of the learning process. Don't let the fear of failure hold you back from achieving your career goals. Instead, embrace failure as an opportunity to learn and grow.

Be Persistent: Persistence is key to achieving your career goals. Keep pushing yourself to improve and never give up on your dreams.

◆ ◆ ◆

Set Career Goals

Identify Your Long-Term Career Goals: Start by identifying your long-term career goals. What do you want to achieve in your career five, ten, or twenty years from now?

Break Down Your Goals into Smaller Steps: Breaking down your goals into smaller steps can help you achieve them more easily. Identify the specific actions you need to take to achieve your long-term career goals.

Set Realistic Deadlines: Setting realistic deadlines can help you stay on track and motivated. Make sure your deadlines are achievable and give yourself enough time to complete each step.

Measure Your Progress: Measuring your progress can help you stay motivated and identify areas where you need to improve. Keep track of your achievements and celebrate your successes along the way.

Achieving your career goals requires hard work, dedication, and a willingness to take risks. By unleashing your inner wolf and setting clear career goals, you can achieve success and fulfillment in your professional life. Remember, the journey to success is not always easy, but it's always worth it.

Discovering the wolf within you can be a transformative journey that leads to personal and professional growth. By embracing your inner wolf, you can tap into your natural strengths, build your confidence, and achieve your goals.

To unleash your inner wolf, start by identifying your strengths and weaknesses. This self-reflection will allow you to hone your skills and work on areas where you need improvement. Developing your instincts and intuition is also crucial. By trusting yourself and practicing mindfulness, you can better navigate difficult situations and make confident decisions.

As a wolf leader, you can inspire others and create a positive workplace culture by embodying the characteristics of successful wolf leaders. By building trust and respect and fostering collaboration, you can outsmart the competition and achieve your career goals.

Remember to stay fearless in the pursuit of your dreams. Take strategic risks, innovate and adapt to change, and always push yourself to grow and learn. With commitment, perseverance, and a willingness to embrace your inner wolf, you can achieve anything you set your mind to.

So go out there and unleash the wolf within!

wolf

The key to unleashing your inner wolf is to embrace your unique strengths and talents, develop your instincts and intuition, and overcome fear and hesitation. Successful wolf leaders build trust and respect, create a positive and productive workplace culture, and outsmart the competition through strategic thinking and planning, leveraging their unique talents and skills, and innovating and adapting to change.

To achieve your career goals, it's essential to discover the wolf within by embracing your inner strengths, developing your leadership skills, and outsmarting the competition. With persistence, dedication, and commitment, you can unlock your full potential and achieve the success you deserve.

Remember, unleashing your inner wolf is a journey, not a destination. It takes time, patience, and hard work, but the rewards are well worth it.

Keep pushing yourself to grow, develop, and learn, and you'll be well on your way to becoming the best version of yourself.

www.ingramcontent.com/pod-product-compliance
Lightning Source LLC
Chambersburg PA
CBHW070908220526
45466CB00005B/2168